GOODBYE
30s

CELEBRATE ONE DECADE AS
YOU STEP INTO THE NEXT

HELLO
40s

First published in the United Kingdom in 2022 by
Pavilion
43 Great Ormond Street
London
WC1N 3HZ

ISBN: 978-1-191168-2073

A CIP catalogue record for this book is available from the British Library.

10 9 8 7 6 5 4 3 2 1
Reproduction by Rival Colour Ltd, UK
Printed and bound by Toppan Leefung, China

www.pavilionbooks.com

GOODBYE

30s

CELEBRATE ONE DECADE AS
YOU STEP INTO THE NEXT

HELLO

40s

A REFLECTIVE JOURNAL

 PAVILION

CELEBRATING A
DECADE IN THE LIFE OF

....

FROM..(DATE)

TO...(DATE)

WELCOME TO
GOODBYE 30s, HELLO 40s

As one decade comes to an end and another one begins, it is time to take a step back, to pause in the rush of life, and reflect.

To consider all that has happened to you over the past 10 years and all that you wish to happen in the decade to come.

It is time to say farewell to a huge chapter in your life so far. A decade that will have been rich with experiences, achievements, life-changing events and people who will have had a profound effect on the shape of your life today and the person you have become.

Now it is time to welcome in the new decade that lies ahead — a brand new chapter in your life story — and create a clear vision for what you want this chapter to be, and a commitment to making it happen.

So, let's get you started by saying a proper farewell to this past decade and get ready to make these next 10 years your best decade yet!

Selina and Vicki x

HOW THIS JOURNAL WORKS

Goodbye 30s, Hello 40s takes you through a step-by-step process to help you say a proper farewell to this past decade in your life as it comes to an end and step into your forties feeling excited for what lies ahead.

The journey begins with you taking a look back at the past 10 years of your life. Focusing on one year at a time, you'll be guided through a series of questions that will help you to recall and record what you got up to that year: your happiest memories, your achievements, the adventures you went on, the challenges you overcame and the lessons you learnt along the way.

Then you will turn towards the decade that lies ahead. A series of questions and exercises will help you get clear on what you need in your life going forward to feel truly happy, fulfilled and at peace. What dreams you want to go after in this next decade, what you want to make happen in your life, how you want to feel and how you want to live.

By the end of the journal you will have in your hands a beautiful keepsake — a record of a whole decade in the story of your life and a vision for what you want to fill your life with over the next 10 years and beyond.

Remember, that this book will be as unique as you are. So there are no right or wrong ways to answer the questions. You might have loads to write for one question and just a line to write for the next. The key is to relax, have fun with it and just see what answers emerge on the page.

So if you're ready, let's get started.

SELF-REFLECTION FEEDS THE SOUL AND AWAKENS OUR DREAMS

GOODBYE
30s

It's time to take a look back at the past 10 years of your life: at all that you've done and all that you've achieved. At the happy times you've enjoyed and the challenges you've overcome. At the adventures you've been on and the lessons you've learnt along the way.

Use your calendar, journals or photos to help remind you of each year — what you got up to, where you were and who you were with. There are no right or wrong answers to any of the questions. You might have just a few lines to write for one question and lots to write for the next. This is your life and your book. So do it your way.

At the end of each year, you'll find a blank page. This is for you to fill with whatever you want. You might want to print out and stick in a 10 x 15cm photo or two square 7.5 x 7.5cm photos. You might have a postcard, invitation or ticket to a memorable event that you want to stick in. Or you might want to use it to write a list of the books you read, places you visited or parties you went to that year.

10 YEARS AGO...TURNING 30

Where were you this time 10 years ago?

How were you feeling about turning 30?

What was going on in your life then?

How did you celebrate your 30th birthday?

30

What were the key milestones, achievements and events in your life that year?

How do you remember feeling in those days and why?

Where were you living?

Who were you living with, if anyone?

Who were the important people in your life then?

What work were you doing and/or how were you spending your days?

What were the hardest moments that year?

What are you proud of yourself for that year?

What were your happiest moments that year?

MEMORIES OF 30

MEMORIES OF 30

31

What were the key milestones, achievements and events in your life that year?

How do you remember feeling in those days and why?

Where were you living?

Who were you living with, if anyone?

Who were the important people in your life then?

What work were you doing and/or how were you spending your days?

What were the hardest moments that year?

What are you proud of yourself for that year?

What were your happiest moments that year?

MEMORIES OF 31

MEMORIES OF 31

32

What were the key milestones, achievements and events in your life that year?

How do you remember feeling in those days and why?

Where were you living?

Who were you living with, if anyone?

Who were the important people in your life then?

What work were you doing and/or how were you spending your days?

What were the hardest moments that year?

What are you proud of yourself for that year?

What were your happiest moments that year?

MEMORIES OF 32

MEMORIES OF 32

33

What were the key milestones, achievements and events in your life that year?

How do you remember feeling in those days and why?

Where were you living?

Who were you living with, if anyone?

Who were the important people in your life then?

What work were you doing and/or how were you spending your days?

What were the hardest moments that year?

What are you proud of yourself for that year?

What were your happiest moments that year?

MEMORIES OF 33

MEMORIES OF 33

34

What were the key milestones, achievements and events in your life that year?

How do you remember feeling in those days and why?

Where were you living?

Who were you living with, if anyone?

Who were the important people in your life then?

What work were you doing and/or how were you spending your days?

What were the hardest moments that year?

What are you proud of yourself for that year?

What were your happiest moments that year?

MEMORIES OF 34

MEMORIES OF 34

35

What were the key milestones, achievements and events
in your life that year?

How do you remember feeling in those days and why?

Where were you living?

54

Who were you living with, if anyone?

Who were the important people in your life then?

What work were you doing and/or how were you spending your days?

What were the hardest moments that year?

What are you proud of yourself for that year?

What were your happiest moments that year?

MEMORIES OF 35

MEMORIES OF 35

36

What were the key milestones, achievements and events in your life that year?

How do you remember feeling in those days and why?

Where were you living?

Who were you living with, if anyone?

Who were the important people in your life then?

What work were you doing and/or how were you spending your days?

What were the hardest moments that year?

What are you proud of yourself for that year?

What were your happiest moments that year?

MEMORIES OF 36

MEMORIES OF 36

37

What were the key milestones, achievements and events in your life that year?

How do you remember feeling in those days and why?

Where were you living?

Who were you living with, if anyone?

Who were the important people in your life then?

What work were you doing and/or how were you spending your days?

What were the hardest moments that year?

What are you proud of yourself for that year?

What were your happiest moments that year?

MEMORIES OF 37

MEMORIES OF 37

38

What were the key milestones, achievements and events in your life that year?

How do you remember feeling in those days and why?

Where were you living?

Who were you living with, if anyone?

Who were the important people in your life then?

What work were you doing and/or how were you spending your days?

What were the hardest moments that year?

What are you proud of yourself for that year?

What were your happiest moments that year?

MEMORIES OF 38

MEMORIES OF 38

39

What were the key milestones, achievements and events in your life that year?

How do you remember feeling in those days and why?

Where were you living?

Who were you living with, if anyone?

Who were the important people in your life then?

What work were you doing and/or how were you spending your days?

What were the hardest moments that year?

What are you proud of yourself for that year?

What were your happiest moments that year?

MEMORIES OF 39

MEMORIES OF 39

THE LONGER I LIVE, THE MORE BEAUTIFUL LIFE BECOMES

LOOKING BACK AT YOUR 30s

What are you grateful for having happened in your life over the past 10 years?

What are the biggest lessons you are grateful for having learned over the past 10 years?

Who are you grateful for having had in your life over the past 10 years?

What are you grateful to yourself for over the past 10 years?

What will your 30s be remembered for in the story of your life?

What message of love and support would you send back to your 30-year-old self, embarking on your 30s?

HELLO

40s

YOUR LIFE TODAY

Where are you now as you step into your 40th year?

Where are you living?

Who are you living with, if anyone?

Who are the important people in your life?

What work are you doing and/or how do you spend
your days?

What is making you happiest in your life at the moment?

What and who are you grateful for in your life today?

How are you feeling about turning 40?

How are you celebrating your 40th birthday?

DESIGNING A LIFE YOU LOVE IN YOUR 40s

A whole new decade lies ahead of you. A fresh new chapter that is ready for you to fill with the things you love: the people, the places, the activities and experiences. A new blank canvas for you to create on, as you go after your dreams and design a life you love to live.

So what do you want to fill your life with? What adventures do you want to go on? What dreams would you like to go after? What do you want to create and make happen in this next decade of yours?

Over the next few pages you're going to start creating a list of all the things you'd like to fill your life with in your 40s. You don't need to have the next decade mapped out ahead of you (in fact please don't try to do that!), but it can feel wonderful to get clear on what you want more of in your life, some of the dreams you want to go after and how you want to feel.

So that, as you step into your 40s, you do so feeling excited about what lies ahead and recognising the power you have to be the artist of your own life, with a clear list of ingredients of what you want to fill your life with in the years to come. Ingredients that will bring you joy, happiness, peace and fulfilment.

As with the previous section, there are no right or wrong answers to any of these questions. You might have loads to write on one and just a sentence to write on the next. And don't worry if you find yourself repeating some answers. It simply helps to highlight some ingredients that are particularly important to you.

So relax your mind, let your imagination go and see what emerges on the page in front of you as you start to write...

FILLING YOUR 40s WITH THE THINGS THAT MAKE YOU HAPPY

What do you love to do?

What are the activities that make you come alive
(at home, at work or on holiday)?

What do you want to do more of in your 40s?

What do you want to do less of in your 40s?

DAY-TO-DAY HAPPINESS

What's your favourite way to start the day?

What's your favourite way to end the day?

What do you want to do more of in your 40s to help you enjoy your day-to-day life?

What do you want to do less of in your 40s to help you enjoy your day-to-day life?

WHAT ARE THE PLACES YOU LOVE TO SPEND TIME IN?

What places (or kinds of places) do you most enjoy spending time in?

What places do you want to spend more time in in your 40s?

What places do you want to spend less time in in your 40s?

What new places do you want to visit?

WHAT DO YOU WANT TO GET UP TO IN YOUR 40s?

What do you want to create, achieve or make happen in your 40s?

What adventures do you want to go on?

What challenges do you want to take on in your 40s?

What do you want to learn?

What life do you dream of?

If you had a magic wand, what would you make happen in your life in your 40s?

What places would you live in?

What would your home(s) be like?

What kind of work or projects would you do?

What would a typical day in your life look like?

What kind of holidays would you go on?

Who would the special people in your life be?

How would it feel to be living that life?

What part of that dream life would you love to focus on turning into your reality over the next few years?

How do you want to feel in your 40s?

Circle one to three feelings you'd most like to feel as you enter into your 40s, adding any that you don't see written below:

happy • joyful • peaceful • content • full of love
connected • serene • energised • playful
fun-loving • grateful • in flow • excited • alive
full of wonder • fulfilled • free • at ease
full of purpose • nourished • relaxed
rested • focused • inspired

In my 40s, I want to feel

....

....

What activities, places, people or practices help you to feel that way?

LET YOUR 40s BE THE DECADE WHEN YOU MAKE YOUR DREAMS COME TRUE

COMMIT TO THE LIFE
YOU WANT TO LIVE

Designing a life you love doesn't happen by accident. Whatever your dreams, your desires, your visions for the life you want to be living are, it isn't luck that will make them happen. It is you committing to those dreams and taking action to bring them to life, that will ultimately have you creating and living a life you love in the next decade and beyond.

And so, now that you know what ingredients you need in your life to feel happy, at peace and fulfilled, it is time to commit to filling your life with those ingredients, following your dreams and creating a life you love as you step into a brand new decade.

So let's get you doing that...

NOW I AM 40...

Now I am 40 I promise to fill my life with the things that help me to feel...

....

....

....

I promise to spend more time...

....

....

....

And less time...

....

....

....

I will aim to start my day with...

....

....

....

I will aim to end my day with...

....

....

....

I will spend as much time as I can in the places I love, such as

....

....

....

I promise to fill my life doing the things that make me truly happy, such as

....

....

....

And I commit to going after my dreams of...

....

....

....

Signed

....

TIME TO STEP INTO A
BRAND NEW DECADE

And so, you are now ready to step forward into a brand new decade, clear on the ingredients you wish to fill it with, how you want to feel, the adventures you want to go on and the dreams you want to bring to life.

Remember always that this is your life.

It is entirely up to you how you live it.

Make your happiness and wellbeing a top priority in your life.

Come back regularly to remind yourself of the commitments you have made to yourself.

Forgive yourself and recommit.

Designing a life you love takes practice, commitment and recommitment.

You'll fall off track from time to time. We all do.

But when that happens, don't beat yourself up.

Forgive yourself and recommit to filling your life with the things you love and the dreams you want to make come true.

And, step by step, you'll find yourself creating a life you love living.

YOUR 40s ARE WAITING FOR YOU. GO AND FILL THEM WITH A LIFE YOU LOVE

NOTES

NOTES

NOTES

NOTES

NOTES

NOTES

NOTES